Li

Expatriate

A Biography of Ezra Pound

By Paul Brody

BookCaps™ Study Guides

www.bookcaps.com

© 2014. All Rights Reserved.

Cover Image © artcalin - Fotolia.com

Table of Contents

ABOUT LIFECAPS 3

INTRODUCTION 4

CHAPTER 1: EARLY LIFE AND CAREER **5**
   EDUCATION 11
   ROMANCE AND INFATUATIONS 15
   GRADUATE SCHOOL AND TEACHING 16
   TO EUROPE 19

CHAPTER 2: LONDON **23**
   LITERARY SOCIETY 25
   MORE TRAVELS: ITALY AND THE US 33
   RETURN TO EUROPE 36
   THE NEW AGE AND IMAGISM 39
   MARRIAGE TO DOROTHY SHAKESPEAR 47
   VORTICISM 49
   THE WAR YEARS AND LEAVING LONDON 54

CHAPTER 3: PARIS **59**
   CAFÉS, SALONS AND BOOKSTORES 61
   MASTERPIECES 65
   1923 69

CHAPTER 4: ITALY **74**
   WRITING INTO OBSCURITY 75
   HISTORY, POLITICS AND FASCISM 79
   WAR LOOMING 85
   WORLD WAR II AND THE AMERICAN HOUR 88
   THE END 93

CHAPTER 5: WASHINGTON **95**

CHAPTER 6: LAST YEARS IN ITALY **100**

CONCLUSION **104**

BIBLIOGRAPHY **105**

About LifeCaps

LifeCaps is an imprint of BookCaps™ Study Guides. With each book, a lesser known or sometimes forgotten life is is recapped. We publish a wide array of topics (from baseball and music to literature and philosophy), so check our growing catalogue regularly (**www.bookcaps.com**) to see our newest books.

Introduction

Ezra Pound was one of the most important figures of Modernism in English literature. Ironically, it was his work on behalf of other more so than his own contributions that created this reputation. James Joyce, T.S. Eliot and Ernest Hemingway all owed an enormous debt to the redheaded, loudmouthed scholar whose life began on the Idaho frontier. On the other hand, Ezra made barely a dent in the public imagination. Later in life, he was far more notorious for his activities during the Second World War than for anything he had added to literary universe.

Chapter 1: Early Life and Career

Ezra Pound's family line in America went back two hundred years. Both his mother's and father's ancestors emigrated from England in the 17th century, and both had members who exerted significant influence in Colonial society.

Mary Weston, Pound's maternal grandmother, read to him as a boy from both classic and popular novels, and from the pages of the family's history.

Pound's grandfather on his father's side had maybe the most lasting effect on his development from a child into an adult. Thaddeus Pound had spent his life accumulating and then losing huge fortunes. He was at times a schoolteacher, a business owner, and a bookkeeper. He represented his home state of Wisconsin in the United States Congress for three terms, where he rubbed elbows with the most powerful men in the nation. In every sense, Thaddeus Pound was the kind of self-made man that everyone revered in nineteenth century America, not the least of them his young grandson.

Homer Pound did not inherit his father's ambition or intensity; instead, he was quiet, kind and did not leave a strong impression on most people. Born in Wisconsin, Thaddeus wielded his influence, as he often would, to secure his son a position at the prestigious West Point military academy. Homer, though, never completed the trip to New York. He returned to his hometown of Chippewa Falls and took a job in a butcher's shop.

Later, Homer courted and married the beautiful Isabel Weston in Washington. His family name opened doors that would have definitely remained shut otherwise. To ensure the newlyweds had financial stability, Thaddeus arranged for his son to have a civil servant's position in a land management office in the frontier state of Idaho.

Not surprisingly, Pound's father was not cut out to be a land manager in a place like Hailey, Idaho, which was in many ways still as lawless as the mythical Wild West. Homer's job was to record land claims; any citizen could make a claim simply by occupying and working a parcel of land. The free-for-all nature of the Idaho land rush led to countless arguments, many of which were settled at the barrel of a gun. Isabel was even less suited to frontier life. Accustomed to a level of refinement that didn't exist in a mining town, she made no secret that she hated their life as it was.

The family's first and only child, Ezra Weston Loomis Pound, was born on October 30, 1885. When he was 18 months old, Isabel had had enough of Idaho and bundled her son up for the train ride back east; Homer followed soon afterwards. The family first spent six months in Manhattan, living partly on the charity of Isabel's family. Next, they moved back west to northern Wisconsin and resided on Thaddeus's farm. The wanderings came to an end in June 1889, when the family moved to Philadelphia, where Homer's father had again flexed his muscle and created an opportunity for his son.

Homer went to work at the United States Mint in Philadelphia, leveraging the knowledge he acquired assaying gold and other precious metals on the frontier. The Mint became his career; he stayed there for 40 years. After a couple of years in a humble row house, the family purchased a 7-bedroom home in the nearby community of Wyncote. Though not rich themselves, many of their neighbors were distinguished in various sectors of the Philadelphia and East Coast business world. Ezra grew up in comfort and security, but not excessive wealth.

In the summer of 1889, the same year the family settled back east, one of Ezra's rich aunts took him and his mother on a whirlwind three-month tour of Europe and North Africa. The journey made a lasting impression on his young imagination.

Thanks mostly to Isabel, the Pound household was refined and literate, decorated in the standard Victorian style. She often read poetry to her son before nap and bed times. Seeing her only child as a delicate pet, she lavished attention on Ezra and dressed him as prettily as was reasonable for a boy. Homer, meanwhile, participated in civic life with gusto. He was a school board member, superintendent of a local Sunday school and church elder. …

Even at a young age, adults could see that Ezra was a gifted and maybe peculiar child. At six years old, he earned the nickname of "the Professor" at a Quaker school for his startlingly advanced language skills. When he began dressing himself, he soon adopted the habit of dressing with the purpose of standing out in the crowd. Ezra wrote his first poem at age 11 on the subject of political reformer William Jennings Bryan; he likely heard his mother's family in Manhattan discussing Bryan's revolutionary plans to alter the course of the nation's economic systems by disbanding the Federal Reserve. Regular visits to his grandmother's offered him a different perspective on current events than that which he received in Wyncote.

Ezra grew steadily into his own person, but not without absorbing some of his parents' traits and values – or reacting against them with passion. He rebelled in the face of his mother's obsession with manners and adherence to Victorian fashions and social roles. On the other hand, he idolized his kind and uncomplicated father, but probably felt a bit disappointed that Home didn't inherit his own father's unswerving fire and ambition. Ezra was wholeheartedly determined to make the world respect him, one way or another.

Education

Ezra had picked up a great deal of knowledge from his parents and his self-directed readings. He also enjoyed the guidance of elders who saw his potential. At church, for instance, the Reverend Carlos Chester sensed the talent in his young congregant, and encouraged him to study the mysteries of the Bible. Ezra's formal education began at 12 years old when he entered Cheltenham Military Academy. The high expectations of a military establishment were too much for him, though, and he yearned to return to the routine and slower pace of home.

At age 15, Ezra and his mother agreed that he was sufficiently advanced in his education to forego regular schooling and proceed straight into a university. He reported that he had for some time already been absolutely confident of his ultimate goal in life: to become a famous poet. Maybe, he thought, he might even become the most famous poet in history.

Ezra officially enrolled at the University of Pennsylvania in 1901, just short of his sixteenth birthday. His unruly red-and-blond hair and unfashionable style of dress immediately made him stand out from his older peers. And naturally, in such an environment, standing out was not usually a desirable trait. With few friends, he was harassed continually, once being drenched in a cold pond for the offense of wearing red socks.

Scholastically, Ezra did not rise to the top of his class, nor did he sink to the bottom. He was, at first, mostly quiet in lectures. His main handicap was that he wasn't interested in conforming to the expectation that he merely absorb the knowledge presented to him. Even at 16 years of age, Ezra already had a firm idea of what he wanted to get out of his university experience. He primarily sought an exhaustive knowledge of modern languages and poetry. His professors didn't know what to do with that kind of single-minded ambition, and they often clashed.

Among the few friends that Ezra somehow managed to make at Penn was the young medical student and future poet William Carlos Williams. Although in awe of Ezra's passion for literature and languages, Williams soon found he could only handle his friend in relatively small doses. Together, the two played tennis and chess or worked semi-collaboratively on poetry. More often than not, Ezra read his latest works aloud to a befuddled but admiring Williams. In 1903, he was part of the chorus in a production of *Iphigenia Among the Taurans*, a Classical Greek play by Euripedes. Out of all his recreational pursuits, however, Ezra gravitated most strongly toward fencing. On the one hand, he appreciated fencing as an organic art form in its own right. On the other hand, he understood from his own study the important position that fencing held in the medieval tradition of the court.

Ezra also forged a relationship with the painter William Brooke Smith, who initiated his interest in Oscar Wilde's theories on the meaning of art in society. Smith's bohemian, morally questionable group of followers concerned the Pound family so much that they suggested he transfer to another school. Also concerning them was Ezra's mediocre grades. So, in the fall of 1903, Isabel traveled with her son to upstate New York, where he enrolled in the small, rural Hamilton College.

Hamilton was conservative through and through, with the expectation that all students fall in line. But as he had done at Penn, Ezra was the odd one out, and he didn't much care. He suffered through the usual hazing and bullying, but eventually settled into a groove that allowed him to pursue his intended course of study. For the most part, that consisted of modern languages. Several of his teachers contributed meaningfully to his development, unlike those he butted heads with in Philadelphia. William Pierce Shepherd introduced Ezra to Dante, the Italian Renaissance master who would become his lifelong passion. Meanwhile, the Reverend Joseph Darling Ibbotson opened up for him the quiet majesties of Anglo-Saxon; it was during one of their many conversations that Ezra first formed his idea for *The Cantos*.

At Hamilton, Ezra was faced with the difficult task of choosing a career path for his adult life. He entertained the ideas of law and investment banking, then turned to diplomatic work, which would put his language skills to great use. However, he abandoned each of these possible careers, in part because his teachers convinced him that his intellectual refinement made him an ideal candidate for advanced study followed by teaching at a university. At that time, Ezra had set aside many hours of his free time to translate late medieval poetry from the Provençal region of southern France.

Romance and Infatuations

Ezra became hung up one a young woman named Viola Baxter while in upstate New York. However, nothing more substantial than a friendship conducted by letters became of their relationship. A more serious romance bloomed when he first entered Penn; there, he first met 15-year-old Hilda Doolittle, whose father was on the astronomy faculty at the university. The two of them shared an innocent kind of love affair. Later, Doolittle, or H.D. as she was later known, became a de facto student of Ezra. While she was studying at Bryn Mawr, much of her energy was in fact given to following a curriculum laid out for her by Ezra, who she saw as her mentor. He instructed her in both Latin and Greek Classics. And like Ezra, H.D. never quite "fit in" in the world of academia.

H.D. all but worshipped Ezra. The only roadblock to their becoming anything more than close friends was Professor Doolittle, who developed a strong disgust with Ezra based on first impression alone. At any rate, it's improbable that a romantic relationship would have been in H.D.'s best interests. Ezra didn't feel quite as intensely about her as she did about him. The truth of this is borne out in his actions: he maintained flirty correspondences with more than one other woman at the same time. Beside H.D. and Baxter, Ezra was also slyly courting Mary Moore, a plainspoken girl from rural New Jersey.

Graduate School and Teaching

From 1905 to 1907, Ezra pursued graduate studies at the University of Pennsylvania, where he had begun his academic career. Although he was a more committed student this time around, he still thumbed his nose at many things the institution held sacred.

Ezra earned his M.A. after only one year of study. In June 1906, he was awarded the Harrison Fellowship in Romantics. The fellowship came with a generous stipend and tuition. Ezra used the money for a trip to Europe that summer, where the landscape and architecture only helped to reaffirm the value of his intellectual pursuits.

For his dissertation topic, Ezra chose to examine the character of the Fool, as realized in the work of Spanish Renaissance playwright Lope de Vega. Interestingly, he would throughout his life adopt this role, consciously or otherwise, when he wished to tear down the curtains of polite society and its stifling rules and expectations. His willingness to take on this role would have consequences as well.

Further conflicts with Penn faculty members led Ezra to once again question whether the halls of academia were really a place he wanted to spend the bulk of his adult life. Nevertheless, in the summer following his European trip, he cast a wide net in search of teaching positions. He quickly heard back about an opportunity at tiny Wabash College in rural Indiana, which was then in the process of expanding its modern languages course offerings.

Located in the 8,500-person town of Crawfordsville, Wabash College had only about 150 students. Religion and football were the keystones of the insulated and conservative community. The general atmosphere in Crawfordsville had the effect of making Ezra want to stand apart even more than he usually did. His classrooms often became seminars in the study of his own particular interests at the time. Some students complained about his bad language and unconventional teaching style. The college president once reprimanded him for smoking, which was technically forbidden in Crawfordsville.

A light teaching load gave Ezra plenty of time for poetry, reading and writing letters to his female friends. He sent an engagement ring to Mary Moore, who turned him down with the unfortunate news that she had already said "yes" to someone else. The ring Ezra sent just happened to be a gift from another woman, so he could not have been excessively hurt by her rejection. Either way, he began to strongly dislike the confining world of Crawfordsville, where every neighbor kept an eye on every other neighbor.

Ezra attempted to heal his loneliness by assembling a small group of likeminded individuals, but the landlord didn't appreciate the noise and traffic. He also raised eyebrows by flirting with some of the unattached young women in town. On one particular winter evening, he found one of his female admirers cold and alone on the street, and he invited her to stay the night. Of course, the landlords discovered this and quickly informed the college president. Ezra was dismissed as of the end of the current semester. The whole Wabash College experience permanently soured him against the university system; his disgust with the machine of professors and administrators would fuel angry nonfiction pieces for decades to come.

To Europe

With just $80 in his pocket, Ezra left for Europe in February 1908. Taking a cattle boat to save money, he disembarked on the island of Gibraltar. Almost immediately, he began sending poems to some of the leading publications in the States.

By summer, he had more or less settled in Venice, though he still had nothing like steady employment. The watery city was especially evocative for Ezra, as it was a touchstone for many of the medieval poets and artists he was then studying. Much of those first few months were spent exploring the art and architecture of Venice and writing poetry inspired by what he saw. From America came a steady stream of rejection letters. Despite a deflated confidence in what he was doing, he persevered.

For a brief time, Ezra worked as the unpaid European manager of Katharine Ruth Heyman, a professional musician 15 years older than himself. She was one more in a line of infatuations. He dutifully booked shows and even held promotional press conferences, but at some point he made a faux pas, and was requested not to represent Miss Heyman any longer.

Ezra was not without allies in Venice. The Reverend Alex Robertson, a family friend, encouraged him in his pursuits and recommended an affordable printer. There, he produced 100 copies of *A Lume Spento* (translated as *With Tapers Quenched*) with some of the last of his remaining resources. Ezra's first poetry collection was dense with medieval themes and subject matter, and borrowed its title from Dante. He sent the book to H.D. and William Carlos Williams. To his father, he sent 40 copies. What he needed was positive reviews in well-circulated publications. Like many other struggling writers, he composed some of his own reviews under pseudonyms to send to publishers. When London's *Evening Standard* printed a friendly mention of Ezra's poetry collection, he intuitively understood that he needed to go there. As the home of William Butler Yeats, among other luminaries, London presented itself as the place to be for writers at the beginning of their careers.

Chapter 2: London

Ezra's money woes did not disappear simply because he migrated to an English-speaking nation. His first weeks in London were spent bouncing from one cheap hotel to the next and barely eating enough to sustain him. Most of his waking hours were spent writing – he was continuing with his project of testing the limits of modern poetry and ideally discovering his own poetic voice along the way. He sent out more pieces to major literary journals, both in England and America, and received one rejection after another. Homer and Isabel Pound pleaded with their son to return to Philadelphia and seek gainful employment.

With his money nearly exhausted, Ezra found a short-term assignment delivering lectures at Regent Street Polytechnic. Meanwhile, he was assembling and organizing the many pages of poetry that he had written while in Venice. He considered these to be among his best work at the time. A minor breakthrough occurred in October 1908 when the *Evening Standard* published "Histrion," one of his Venice compositions. Written in the style of a dramatic monologue, "Histrion" recalled the work Robert Browning, the noted Victorian poet of the previous century. It's fair to say that much of Ezra's early work echoed the past in this way.

At 23 years of age, Ezra conceived of himself as a genius descended, metaphorically speaking, from a long line of fellow geniuses. His extreme confidence in his own abilities was a distinct part of his character for most of his adult life. Although his early work was imitative, he was so good at it that reviewers rarely found fault with the method. However, Ezra recognized his need to distance himself from his own influences. Between 1908 and 1912, therefore, he self-consciously tried to break out of the mold he had created.

In terms of his artistic debts, Ezra felt most conflicted about Walt Whitman, the 19th century American poet. On the one hand, he acknowledged the importance of Whitman to the poetic tradition before many others. He identified the use of ordinary speech and deeply personal themes and perspectives as a major shift in what poetry could accomplish. On the other hand, Ezra shied away from the idea that poetry ought to speak to the "common" people – workers and farmers, etc.

In December 1908, Ezra published *A Quinzaine for This Yule*. Elkin Mathews, a London publisher who saw potential in the young and brash American, agreed to print this newest collection along with a larger collection that was forthcoming. Both this new collection and his ongoing lectures at Regent Street earned him mentions in the London daily papers; after much struggle, he was starting to get the recognition that he felt he deserved.

Literary Society

In the world of English literature in the early 20th century, few cities compared with London for its concentration of talent. Henry James, Joseph Conrad and Thomas Hardy were the elder statesmen of fiction. H.G. Wells was creating an innovative new genre, science fiction, while George Bernard Shaw dominated the theater. In poetry, however, there was something of a vacuum. The last English poet to fully capture the literary public's imagination was Algernon Swinburne, and his greatest work was a decade or more behind him.

The publisher Elkin Mathews was also the proprietor of a well-known bookshop, where Ezra browsed the shelves with deep interest. The bookshop also became an important meeting place, giving him the chance to strike up professional relationships with poet and novelist Maurice Hewlett and poetry critic Henry Newbolt. In January 1909, Ezra met Frederic Manning, a visiting Australian with a passion for Greek lyric poetry; the two hit it off immediately. Manning then introduced him to Olivia Shakespear and her daughter Dorothy, who he was attempting to romance at the time.

It was instantly obvious that Ezra did not exactly "fit in" with English society. The dry, refined manners of the English highlighted his own quirks, as had been the case in Crawfordsville. Society itself was floating in a kind of limbo between the Victorian and Modern ages. In Europe, the rumblings of war were already apparent to any who were listening. Germany was in the midst of a military buildup, while numerous countries were wracked with civil unrest and political agitation. It seemed that assassinations were happening with a disturbing regularity. Ezra, though, was not yet attuned to political events on the other side of the English Channel. He was far more concerned with getting to the heart of the literary society that he both worshipped and slightly envied.

Beginning in 1909, Ezra was a frequent guest at tea and dinner parties hosted by important figures in the world of letters. He was also invited to private literary societies and clubs, where he rubbed elbows with many people he had idolized from afar, such as Shaw and Hilaire Beloc. Despite these successes, Ezra was still mired in poverty. His father sent enough money to keep him from starving and being utterly homeless, and Olivia Shakespear also contributed to her young friend's maintenance. Meanwhile, Olivia's daughter Dorothy had a different kind of interest in his wellbeing.

Almost from first sight, Dorothy was smitten with Ezra; he was not unaware that he had that effect on women. Only a year younger than Ezra, Dorothy was living at home after completing her education. The pair began a serious and lengthy courtship that was not without complications.

In April, Ezra finally had the chance to meet William Butler Yeats, thanks to the Shakespears, who were acquainted with both. Olivia spoke glowingly of Ezra before the meeting, priming the older Yeats to like the energetic, intense young American poet. The publication of *Personae* was another landmark event that spring. The collection contained many pieces from *A Lume Spento*, along with new material that was likewise rooted in medievalism and obscure historical persons and events. Dedicated to Mary Moor, *Personae* earned him several positive and encouraging reviews. The collection also made possible an encounter with Ford Madox Hueffer – he changed his last name to Ford after World War I – who had many connections to writers of the previous generation. Through Ford, Ezra learned intimate details of life with Dante and Christina Rossetti, Robert Browning and Algernon Swinburne.

Perhaps more importantly for Ezra than his literary ties, Ford was the editor of the *English Review*, then one of the leading arts publications in the English-speaking world. Ezra was understandably drawn to someone so obviously at the heart of all things literary. Expressing confidence in his yet unproven talent, Ford promised to place some of his work in an upcoming issue. "Sestina: Altaforte," a meditation on medieval warfare, appeared in the June 1909 edition of the *English Review*.

By the time of his publication in Ford's magazine, Ezra had found himself a part of a loosely organized group of likeminded writers trying to find new directions in poetry. Other members included its de facto leader, T.E. Hulme, Joseph Campbell and Ernest Rhys. Together, the members of this informal association experimented with new rhyme schemes, free verse and unconventional subject matter.

Ezra's star power was beginning to rise, even if his finances were still grounded. Mathews requested another book from him as soon as practical, while Regent Street offered him another lecture series. Another new friend who would become a strong supporter, Wyndham Lewis, sensed the nervous energy inside Ezra waiting to burst out. A then little-known D.H. Lawrence, on the other hand, found him off-putting and pretentious. As a general rule, everyone who met Ezra fell into two camps – admiration or disgust. Always the self-promoter, not to mention convinced of his own genius, polite English society often saw him as a "charlatan" imported from uncultured America.

In many ways, Ezra modeled his public persona after Whistler, one of his many artistic idols. He saw the much-maligned painter as an exile on behalf of his creative impulse. Ezra's lack of concern for society's approval was on full display when he wrote "The Ballad of Goodly Fere," an irreverent portrait of Jesus and his disciples. The poem was included in *Exultations* against the advice of Mathews, who inserted a disclaimer for readers who might be shocked by its contents.

Exultations, published in September 1909, was showered with more good reviews. Again, the collection was distinctly rooted in the deep past – one reviewer noted this as a potential problem, along with the poet's tendency to distance himself from readers by way of excessive scholarly allusions and language. It was a criticism that would dog Ezra throughout his career.

About the same time *Exultations* came off the presses, Ezra moved to new lodgings in Kensington, just a short walk from the Shakespears, among other friends and associates. In October, he began has lecture series on medieval literature at Regent Street. The series took him through to the following spring. Because the audience was typically composed of people with little formal education, Ezra's discussions went almost entirely over their heads. Compounding that communication barrier was that he made no effort to simplify or streamline his ideas. At the suggestion of Mathews, he started work on turning his lecture notes into a book of literary criticism.

Ezra realized during the long winter of 1909/10 that he needed to pivot away from the stiff and formal classical English that had dominated his poetic voice to something more raw and American. His inspiration for this transition was the Provençal poets who he had long studied. At a time when Latin dominated the Western world, these poets, known also as Troubadors, instead adopted their own vernacular speech for poetry and prose. This epiphany coincided with Ezra's steadily growing fame. By this point, his name was mentioned in significant literary magazines on both sides of the Atlantic. Recognition on this scale was enough to make him consider a return to America, and he applied for a fellowship at Penn.

In March, Ezra was visited by William Carlos Williams, who was then on his way home from Germany. Williams remembered several instances of bad manners, and was not unhappy when it was time to leave his old friend behind in London.

Before leaving London, Ezra managed to get wrapped up in the occult craze that had taken root, especially among the educated and sophisticated classes. Yeats himself believed in the possibility of communing with ghosts. To supposedly get a better understanding of himself and his purpose in life, Dorothy Shakespear completed Ezra's astrological chart.

More Travels: Italy and the US

As spring came to London, Ezra traveled south to Italy, first stopping off in Verona, where Dante composed many of his most famous works, before settling down for an extended stay in the secluded hamlet of Sirmione. He received news that a Boston publisher was keen to release an American edition of his poems, a further enticement to return home. In April, he was joined by the Shakespears. The group traveled to Venice, where Ezra took the ladies to all the most important sites. When Dorothy and Olivia headed back to London, he made his way to Sirmione again to consider his next steps. The idea of reacquainting himself with his American brethren seemed terrifying.

In June 1910, *The Spirt of Romance* was published, establishing in precise language Ezra's thoughts on the history of poetry and aesthetics. No sooner was the book on shelves than he was on a ship heading west across the Atlantic.

Summer in Philadelphia was unpleasant. Ezra suffered from both jaundice and depression and could barely tolerate the presence of his mother. When he felt stronger, he visited all of his old friends and tried to create the kind of intimate circle of intellectuals of which he had been a part in London. He had no luck; in his opinion, America was a vast cultural desert.

When Penn rejected his fellowship application, Ezra gave up any desire to re-enter the academy, which was not particularly strong to begin with. Instead, he focused his energy on translating the work of 12th century Italian poet Cavalcanti, and writing a handful of reviews for various publications. In the fall, he moved to an apartment on Park Avenue in Manhattan, where he soon met Yeats's father. The elderly Yeats introduced Ezra to John Quinn, a lawyer who would later become one of his most valued and faithful patrons.

Having finished his translation work in November, Ezra sent a new collection of poetry to his Boston publisher. *Provenca* received only mixed reviews in the States. At the same time, unknown to Ezra, his London publisher was recommending him to the poet Harriet Monroe. As with Quinn, Monroe would be instrumental in his later success and reputation.

Ezra spent the Thanksgiving holiday in New Jersey at the home of Williams. The two had already begun a decades-long debate over the proper substance of poetry. Whereas Ezra believed that poets should exist in rarefied air and speak to the elites, Williams was more of a populist. Williams likened himself to bread, Ezra to caviar.

Back in New York, Ezra continued to complain about the sad state of affairs in American letters. He was also, sadly, annoyed at the influx of Eastern European and Jewish immigrants, betraying the first inklings of a racism that would later consume him, tarnish his reputation, and even threaten his freedom. The major poets in America at the time were still largely undiscovered and disconnected. Two people tried hard to change that reality. Harriet Monroe founded *Poetry*, and Margaret Anderson began *The Little Review*. Both of these publications would help launch the careers of countless writers over the coming years. Also in 1910, the Poetry Society of America held its first meeting. Ezra attended but did not take the event seriously.

Return to Europe

Downcast and frustrated with the art and literary scenes in the nation of his birth, Ezra returned to England after only six months away. He came back to a world in the midst of change. King Edward VII died in May 1910; technology was advancing at a breathtaking pace, with new inventions coming out all the time – automobiles, motion pictures, X-rays, synthetic fiber and so on. Perhaps the most disturbing advances came in the area of weaponry, though few realized it at the time. Ezra felt these changes happening all around him, driving him to push his own art form out of stagnation and into the modern age.

The King's death opened the door for all sorts of new reformist and even revolutionary political impulses to gain a foothold. The Fabians, for example, believed that democracy was decadent and that people ought to be ruled by a class of "experts." The leading Fabians published the tenets of their "rational socialist state" in leading fringe publications. Ezra was energized and swept up by the new politics. He was even more entranced by the remarkable turn of events in the world of painting. Arriving back in the city just in time to see the infamous Grafton Gallery show, where the most famous of the French Post-Impressionists displayed their newest creations, he saw how far painting had moved beyond the models of the previous century. Ezra believed firmly that poetry needed to move in the same direction.

Naturally, the Grafton Gallery show, among other displays of Modernism in the arts, provoked a strong and swift reaction from social conservatives. Politicians and religious leaders denounced the immorality of the French painters and warned British society to resist their influence. Novels were likewise condemned for encouraging unspoken sexual crimes. In the streets, however, a liberalizing spirit was everywhere to be felt. Women wore shorter skirts and brighter colors, and ordinary citizens discussed matters openly that had always been taboo.

Feeling an urge to get out of London for the summer, Ezra traveled south to Paris, where he attempted to put his finger on the pulse of Modern Art. He noted that many painters were dampening their color palettes, choosing to work in browns and blacks. He then toured a few of his favorite locales in Italy before heading north to visit Ford in Germany. Ford had traveled there with his mistress, Violet Hunt, hoping to get a divorce from his wife; he was unsuccessful. Ezra showed him a copy of his newest and still-unpublished collection *Canzoni*. Ford was unimpressed, accusing the poet of falling back on the habits of old and dead writers. Ezra could not disagree.

The New Age and Imagism

As summer came to an end, Ezra was back in London. He shifted from one lodging to another while waiting for his room at Church Walk to become vacant. At one of T.E. Hulme's evening gatherings, he met the editor of *The New Age*, A.R. Orage. The encounter was profitable for Ezra – Orage agreed to have him contribute regular articles to the magazine. Covering art, literature and politics, *The New Age* was exactly the kind of platform that appealed to the young American. The magazine deliberately invited controversy by giving a voice to society's most radical elements. Ezra earned 1 pound a week and eventually wrote about 300 articles for Orage's magazine.

Ezra's first contribution to *The New Age* was a creative translation of an Anglo-Saxon poem, "The Seafarer." About the same time, he was becoming intrigued by Oriental art and literature, thanks in part to the enthusiasm of some new acquaintances. Through Orage, he met Allen Upward, a scholar of Oriental art and design; Ezra also read Laurence Binyon's *The Flight of the Dragon*. His interests focused on Chinese and Japanese poetry. Upward communicated some philosophical ideas that would become important to Ezra's development as a poet and thinker, such as "slowness is beauty," a concept that had special significance in a world that seemed always to be accelerating. At the same time, he also learned to appreciate the unique qualities of sculpture, befriending the impoverished but outgoing Gaudier, whose ramshackle studio stood underneath train tracks.

The New Age became the soapbox upon which Ezra announced and clarified his ideas of what English literature should be in the 20th century. Apart from poems and translations, many of his early contributions were extended essays on the purpose and meaning of poetry, and how critics should approach the medium. At the time, so-called Georgian poetry was captivating the popular imagination. Spearheaded by Edward Marsh, the Georgians were a continuation of the voice and style of the 1890s Romantic poets. For that reason, Ezra believed they had to be challenged.

In the spring of 1911, a brief trip to Paris inspired the first poem that could be categorized as belonging to Imagism, a movement not yet crystallized in Ezra's mind. "In a Station of the Metro" was only two lines and evoked the Japanese haiku format. He reportedly spent a year revising and perfecting its imagery.

As Ezra was opening up new territory in poetry, evenings with Hulme became strained. Both men had powerful personalities, and both wanted to be leaders of whatever new movement in literature emerged from their group conversations. Another complication in Ezra's personal life arose when Olivia Shakespear tried to throw cold water on his growing affection for her daughter Dorothy. Henry Hope Shakespear was far from confident that the young American's career in letters was sustainable for the long haul. For her part, Dorothy quietly encouraged Ezra to ask for her hand in marriage.

The doubts of the Shakespears were misplaced. After many years of true struggle, Ezra was beginning to see his income grow alongside his reputation. The publisher Steven Swift, who had an interest in the avant garde movement in arts, paid him 100 pounds annually in return for a single collection of original poetry or translations. The first few months of 1912, therefore, were occupied with revising the poems that would become *Ripostes*, a breakthrough collection for Ezra. *Ripostes* revealed a new voice, one not reliant on the models and techniques of the past century.

Hilda Doolittle arrived as Ezra was working on his newest poems, and he helped her to get settled, taking her to dinner and tea parties and introducing her to the important people. In some ways, he dominated her time and attention, though she didn't resist him. But Ezra's affections were spread among more than one young woman. In June, feeling abandoned, Margaret Cravens took her own life. Friends secretly blamed Ezra for her death, and he blamed himself as well. He fled the heat and intensity of London to take a walking tour in Provence, clearing his mind as much as possible of the guilt and depression that had bogged him down since Cravens' death.

In August, Ezra was able to move back into his familiar and conveniently situated apartment at Church Walk. The Cubists had begun to commandeer the art scene in Paris, but their influence had not yet reached English shores. Meanwhile, Harriet Monroe had secured enough capital to finally launch her new publication, *Poetry*. She sent a letter to Ezra, among others, asking for contributions. He immediately seized the opportunity. Descended from former US President James Monroe, Harriet Monroe was wealthy and well connected; earning a spot on the pages of her magazine would be an enormous win.

Ezra did what he could to prepare Monroe for his contributions. He explained that his perspective of modern poetry was anything but conventional and some even found him offensive. Monroe had wealth, but that didn't mean she could print anything she wanted. She still had to consider the magazine's backers and the reading public.

The delicate tastes of the reading public were the last thing on Ezra's mind in 1912; in fact, he nurtured a deepening anger toward ordinary people, who he saw as at least partly responsible for the success of "bad art." For *Poetry*, he gathered together some like-minded associates to contribute, making sure that everyone was writing in roughly the same clean style that he had first deployed in "In a Station of the Metro." Technically, the new movement still had no name.

Ripostes was published in October but failed to make waves. The publisher went bankrupt, robbing Ezra of a sure source of income. Perturbed by these failures, he spent Christmas in the North of England with Ford, Violet Hunt and the novelist Compton Mackenzie and his wife. Ezra spent an entire night speaking endlessly on literary topics, showing some early signs of the manic energy that would work against him later in life. Despite the failure of his most recent collection, his reputation, especially in the context of the new movement he was leading, was such that fellow poets came to him at Church Walk for advice and help with revisions.

Ezra's fledgling movement in modern poetry finally earned a name of its own. An early issue of *Poetry* discussed the principles of "Imagism." They included a precise and direct approach to the subject matter, the removal of unnecessary language, little or no abstraction, and the use of free verse. Ezra believed firmly that relying on traditional meters and schemes in poetry was the equivalent of forcing an idea into a predetermined shape, which naturally lessened the impact of the idea. He was conflicted, therefore, when he met Robert Frost in the spring of 1913. The ideas that Frost put on paper were interesting, but Ezra felt his choice of form was misguided.

Spring 1913 saw the publication of several conversational poems from Ezra in *Poetry*, but friction between himself and Monroe was growing. The backers had no interest in his edgier material. Seeking an outlet for his authentic voice, he struck up a relationship with the editors of *The New Freewoman*; they gave him a literary section of his own, with no strict guidelines on what he could or couldn't do with it. What Ezra didn't know then was that his Imagism movement was already in the process of slipping away from him. That summer, Amy Lowell came to London intent on meeting all of the most-esteemed poets and making a career for herself. Her ambition was reinforced by her substantial wealth.

Lowell and Ezra did not meet immediately. Instead, he and a group of other writers spent most of that summer at South Lodge, the home of Violet Hunt. The spacious home became an informal writer's retreat, with guests sharing notes and staying up all hours. Ezra had convinced the editors of *The New Freewoman* to change the name to *The Egoist*, improving its marketability. The bulk of his energy at South Lodge was spent in long discussion with Ford, whom he admired more than nearly anyone he had met in London.

In October, Ezra attended the wedding of Hilda Doolittle and Richard Aldington, then traveled west to spend part of the winter with Yeats in the countryside. He taught the older writer the finer points of fencing and helped him to see the needless wordiness and overly sentimental style of his earlier writing. When he asked if he knew of any up-and-coming Irish poets, Yeats suggested James Joyce, who was then living in Italy. After reading just one piece by Joyce, Ezra wrote to the young man asking permission to publish him in *Des Imagistes*, an anthology he was then producing.

Marriage to Dorothy Shakespear

In the spring of 1914, Ezra's social sphere had contracted somewhat; much of his time was spent with the sculptor Gaudier and fellow writer Wyndham Lewis. Both were considered not quite reputable persons with which to associate oneself. One reason that Ezra didn't care about his friends' social standing was that his long courtship with Dorothy Shakespear seemed to be at an end. The resistance of her parents was looking less and less likely to end. Olivia even suggested that he leave England because he clearly wasn't gentlemanly material. At the same time, she harbored a secret fear that her daughter would never marry; at 27 years old, Dorothy was on the verge of eclipsing marriageable age.

Then, the Shakespears relented, almost overnight. They saw that their daughter's affections were too strong to be denied. Henry Hope sent a letter to Ezra requiring that the marriage be held in a church, a point that he initially refused, but later came round to the older man's wishes. It was not the first or last point of friction between Ezra and his soon-to-be in-laws.

On April 20, 1914, Dorothy and Ezra were married in St. Mary Abbots Church in front of only six guests, one of whom was the jilted and jealous Frederic Manning. Dorothy's parents gifted her a sum of 150 pounds a year that, when combined with Ezra's earnings, would enable them to live relatively comfortably. The newlyweds spent a pleasant honeymoon at Stone Cottage, where Dorothy sketched while Ezra worked on translations and adaptations of Japanese dramatic texts.

Vorticism

Ezra's relationship with Lewis was testy and complicated. At first, the two men didn't exactly trust each other. It was a few years in fact before they considered themselves friends. Lewis was extremely shy but also a little explosive and moody. He deliberately kept people at a distance and enjoyed being thought of as a misanthrope. Ezra penetrated this shell only after repeated attempts. What they had most in common was an ability to thumb their noses at conventions, being rude and classless when situations called for good manners and politeness.

By 1914, Lewis, Ezra and several fellow artists and writers were holding sessions at the Cave of the Golden Calf, an underground club frequented by the avant garde. They positioned themselves as the antidote to the socially acceptable literature then being produced by the Bloomsbury group, headed up by Virginia and Leonard Woolf.

In the months leading up to the Great War, several seemingly divergent movements in art came together in Ezra's imagination. The artists who came together at the Cave represented a new movement that he eventually labeled Vorticism. For Ezra, Vorticism was another step away from the gentle realism of the Victorian era. Even though he guided the movement and pulled fellow artists into its circle, once again it was T.E. Hulme who best expressed its key principles. The anxiety and dissonance of summer 1914 naturally produced an avant garde art movement that communicated those feelings, but most of the general public was not paying attention.

Lewis and Ezra were likewise fascinated by the Futurist movement, then championed by the fiery Italian F.T. Marinetti. The manifesto of Futurism revolved around violence, revolution, destruction and misogyny. In many ways, the movement was a precursor of the Fascist political movement that would grip Italy following the First World War. Ezra personally gravitated Futurism's rejection of the status quo in art and culture. At some points, his tantrums went even too far for Lewis. In an open letter, Ezra challenged the Georgian poet Abercrombie to a duel, though the plan was never carried out.

In the meantime, Lewis founded the Rebel Art Centre to give a chance for his fellow artists to express themselves more freely. Ezra was beginning to sense the limitations of Imagism even in the realm of poetry. He saw that his short, evocative poems could never carry the weight of political or social importance, which was becoming more important to him as he aged. By incorporating elements of Expressionism, Futurism and Cubism, Vorticism captured the frenzy of the pre-war atmosphere. It was a fully interdisciplinary movement too, with poets, sculptors and painters all experimenting along the same general lines. For Ezra, Vorticism gave him the opportunity to begin thinking seriously about a longer project. He knew that he wasn't cut out for writing a novel, but a long-form or multi-part poem might be more manageable. It was from these brainstorms that *The Cantos* eventually emerged.

June 1914 saw the first public announcement of Vorticism as a coherent movement. Lewis gathered contributors together for the publication of BLAST!, a diverse assortment of art, poetry and essays. Critics and the public barely noticed, or saw the movement as a huge joke. Ezra had high hopes for the movement, intending to start a workshop-style institute where Vorticist aesthetic principles would be taught by masters. The plan was too bizarre and impractical for its time.

Ezra's contributions to BLAST! were rage-filled and baffling to his friends who knew him as generally friendly. In his writing, though, he was becoming more and more unsettled by the events of the world, both geopolitically and on the smaller scale. The one stabilizing presence in his life was Dorothy. Because they had enjoyed such a long courtship, their marriage was less passionate than quiet and peaceful. Friends and associates came together to provide the couple with décor and furnishings for their new shared apartment. When not working on his own projects, Ezra and Dorothy studied Chinese together.

As the war in Europe lurched into motion, Amy Lowell returned to London, eager to take a position at the top of whatever arts movement was then underway. She organized a dinner for Ezra and his friends, during which they mercilessly made fun of her. Lowell's ambition was to put out a new anthology of Imagist literature, but this time without Ezra in the role of editor and curator. The anthology would be geared toward American audiences and therefore have an American sensibility.

Having already moved on to Vorticism, Ezra didn't fight Lowell over the "ownership" of Imagism; after she began publishing her own anthologies, he began referring to the movement as "Amygisme." He saw her incarnation as completely void of the energy and purity of the Imagism of 1909-12. Ezra was then much more interested in the work of James Joyce, who had battled for nearly ten years to publish his short story collection, *Dubliners*. He worked on Joyce's behalf to see the book published, and was again impressed when he read the first chapter of *Portrait of the Artist as a Young Man*. Ezra was consistently willing to set aside whatever he was doing to help a fellow artist whom he considered deserving to grab their share of recognition.

Ezra's generous spirit was again called into service by a visiting American, Conrad Aiken. Aiken was shopping around some poems by his Harvard friend, T.S. Eliot. Ezra was astonished by what he read, in particular "The Love Song of J. Alfred Prufrock." Eliot first met his American counterpart in September 1914, after he had left Germany because of the war.

The War Years and Leaving London

Ezra was so heavily absorbed in his own projects that the Great War did not at first attract his attention, despite many friends and acquaintances volunteering for duty on the Continent. He and Dorothy spent the first winter of the war with Yeats at Stone Cottage reading and translating Confucius. The reality of the conflict was not brought home to him until the death of Gaudier in June 1915. The poet Rupert Brooke and philosopher T.E. Hulme would also be swallowed up by the trenches. Ezra tried to volunteer, but his nationality and questionable reputation kept him in England. Given the wartime climate and necessary rationing of basic supplies, the demand for literature was completely sapped.

In April 1915, Ezra completed *Cathay*, a collection of inspired translations from Chinese poetry. The clean and lyrical poems in *Cathay* represent a successful fusion of Imagism with a more straightforward narrative structure. Despite being one of his most coherent and elegant collections to date, the book was ignored. A follow-up collection, *Lustra*, resulted in even more disappointment. The publisher Elkin Mathews resisted printing the collection, claiming it was too indecent even for him.

That same year, Ezra began casual negotiations with John Quinn to stage a Vorticist show in New York. Ezra hinted that life might be easier for both of them if Quinn could offer a small stipend in support of his curating efforts. The New York lawyer agreed, sending him regular cash installments. From Ezra's perspective, having a bona fide "patron" was the fulfillment of one of his early ambitions. His now steadier income enabled him to dedicate more time and energy to a new project that would take up the rest of his life – *The Cantos*.

Ezra worked on the first three sections of *The Cantos* throughout the winter of 1916/17. Harriet Monroe agreed to publish them after some careful editing. In the meantime, Ezra went to great lengths to ensure the ongoing war didn't separate him from the people he held most dear. "The Men of 1914," a term coined by Wyndham Lewis, included Lewis, Ezra, James Joyce and T.S. Eliot. In the summer of 1917, Ezra spent mostly his own funds to see that "The Love Song of J. Alfred Prufrock" was published.

Meanwhile, back in New York, Quinn had thrown his financial weight into a new literary magazine, *The Little Review*. Margaret Anderson and Jane Heap managed the editorial desk in the States, while Ezra was given the title of foreign editor. Although he respected Anderson, their relationship turned sour quickly. His championing of work like Joyce's *Ulysses* ruined any chance to influence American tastes.

A Spanish flu outbreak in 1918 added insult to the injury of war, actually killing more people worldwide than the war had. The conditions of trench warfare and crowded combat ships helped the disease to grow to pandemic proportions. The warring nations had become completely disillusioned after four years of seemingly pointless conflict. The trenches barely moved, and the ravaged landscape was alien and lifeless. The fighting ended on November 11; a million British soldiers had been killed.

The end of the war did little to revive the arts in Britain or elsewhere. A.R. Orage gave up his position at *The New Age*, handing control off to Major Clifford Hugh Douglas. Following Douglas's lead, the magazine began focusing almost exclusively on economic issues. Ezra continued to send articles and reviews, intrigued by the new discussions. One of Douglas's recurring themes was the idea of social credit as opposed to the market economies and centralized currencies of Western democracies. Ezra especially gravitated to the conspiracy theories that put Jewish bankers in control of the world's destiny. The end of the Great War effectively market a turning point in his development, when he began to concentrate less on art and more on politics and sociology, with undertones of paranoia.

With London society totally apathetic where the arts were concerned, Ezra sensed that his time there was limited. He worked on a new poem, "Hugh Selwyn Mauberly," that succinctly captured the downcast spirit of the times from the perspective of defeated artist. In the spring of 1919, Ezra and Dorothy went to Paris for a second honeymoon and took a walking tour in the south of France. On the way home, they were stopped in port by a customs official demanding passports. The ease with which people crossed national borders in Europe before the war was gone forever; Ezra was incensed.

After some bureaucratic wrangling, the Pounds were back in London, where Ezra set to work on sections V, VI and VII of *The Cantos*. He considered a return to America where he might work for a publishing firm in New York, but the idea just seemed intolerable. Critics in America were even less receptive to his art than they were in England, singling out his tendencies for over-sophistication and obscurity. As a new decade dawned, Ezra knew only that he could not stay in London much longer.

In May 1920, Ezra and Dorothy took a European tour, during which they carefully considered where next to set down roots. Ezra had been in London for a dozen years already, and never broke through into the popular imagination as he had hoped. The couple traveled to Paris, Milan and Venice, then to the familiar hideaway of Sirmione. While resting in the mountains, he asked Joyce to come for a visit. Despite being his loudest advocate for several years, the two men had never met. Joyce overcame his dislike of traveling for the sake of his friendship with Ezra.

Chapter 3: Paris

Ezra and Dorothy Pound left London for Paris near the end of 1920. The city was familiar to Ezra, but he had never lived there permanently. He discovered that Paris was generally more engaged with the arts world than London had ever been. The atmosphere was rejuvenating, and he felt liberated like never before. He especially appreciated the international flair to the arts scene, and the ease with which artists from many different disciplines mixed.

War had not stifled the creative energies of the City of Lights, even when the trenches approached to within a few dozen miles. One of the most successful and representative wartime collaborations was *Parade*, a ballet written by Jean Cocteau, scored by Erik Satie and with sets and props designed by Pablo Picasso. It was the sort of collaborative experimentation that Ezra saw as the future trajectory of modern art. Cocteau labeled the work "surrealism."

Another movement coming out of the war years was Dadaism, which attempted to undermine all the cherished notions about what art and culture were supposed to be; the Dadaists found art in everyday objects and injected humor into all of their work. Tristan Tzara was at the forefront of the movement, having helped to launch it in Zurich, Switzerland. Tzara and Ezra became fast friends.

Around Christmas 1920, Ezra found a suitable apartment for Dorothy and himself at 70 rue Notre Dame des Champs. He arranged for his sizable collection of sculptures, paintings and books to be shipped over from London. In the meantime, he and Dorothy spent the first three months of the New Year in the south of France. The exchange rate in France was extremely favorable for living on the cheap. Dorothy's income was more than enough to support them, and anything Ezra earned allowed them to enjoy some luxuries, like eating out frequently. Despite his love for his Irish homeland, James Joyce was convinced of the practicality of living in Paris, and so moved himself about the same time as the Pounds. Ezra also wrote to Ford Madox Ford to praise French living and encourage him to pull up stakes.

The publication of *The Little Review* in New York came to an end after the magazine was convicted of obscenity for printing excerpts from *Ulysses*. Editors Margaret Anderson and Jane Heap didn't want to let the magazine die, so they relocated to Paris, where censors wouldn't be so quick to interfere. Their relationship with Ezra thawed, and he was brought on as an assistant editor. In one of the first issues published from France, he announced the end of the Christian era and the beginning of the Pound era.

Cafés, Salons and Bookstores

In Paris, the cafés were the meeting places for young members of the avant garde. At the Dome café, Ezra met the sculptor Brancusi. He was in awe of the Romanian's command of simple forms, seeing in his work that continuation of what the late Gaudier had begun. Eager to boost his new friend's reputation, Ezra organized a special issue of *The Little Review* to put his work front and center. He even took up sculpting himself, filling the empty spaces of his apartment with small stone objects. At another café, Ezra met the American sculptor Nancy McCormack, only just arrived from New York. She agreed to make a plaster mold of his face that came to be known as his "death mask," one of the more famous artifacts from Ezra's life.

Salons were the counterpart to cafés in 1920s Paris. Typically held at people's homes, the famous salons of Paris were naturally more exclusive than any café. Among the more well-known salons was that of Natalie Barney, whose home on rue Jacob was the frequent destination of the most controversial artists of the period. Ezra once took William Carlos Williams there for a visit, but he was unimpressed. Another leading figure was Coco Chanel, who rose from poverty to become a fashion icon. Her fame began in her own salon, where she entertained designers and intellectuals.

The socially liberated atmosphere of Paris encouraged Ezra to be even more flamboyant, letting his hair grow wild and trimming his beard in curious shapes. He developed an affinity for unusual hats and was often remembered wearing a sombrero. He mixed and matched styles in a way to ensure that he always stood out from the crowd.

Other than the salons and cafés, Sylvia Beach's bookstore, Shakespeare and Company, would be an important way station not only for Ezra, but for every notable artist who resided in or passed through Paris in the 1920s. On the bookstore shelves one could find Ezra alongside Yeats, Eliot and Gertrude Stein. Eager to once more help a friend, Ezra arranged a meeting between Beach and Joyce. Although he didn't make the best first impression, Beach was fascinated enough by the shy Irishman to take up his cause. She offered to publish *Ulysses* on her own dime.

Meanwhile, when not devoting himself to friends, Ezra was hard at work on his own projects. *The Cantos* were still being steadily developed. He had also begun an opera, *Le Testament*, based on the French poet François Villon. The remainder of Ezra's free time was taken up with meeting and entertaining guests. One of these was the young American poet e.e. cummings, who had grown up reading and admiring him. cummings spent the last months of the war in prison after being falsely accused by the French authorities of espionage. Ezra, on the other hand, was a strong admirer of the painter Francis Picabia, who reminded him of Wyndham Lewis and the Vorticists.

Ezra's patron, John Quinn, began expressing frustration with him because of all the time and energy he was giving to associates rather than himself. In an arts capital like Paris, though, it was nearly impossible to sequester oneself. At any rate, conversations and exchanges over the purpose and ultimate direction of art were important to Ezra's creative process. It wasn't enough for him to simply have time alone.

During his first journeys in France, Ezra had developed an appreciation for both the Symbolists and the troubadour poets of Provence. In 1921, he translated Remy de Gourmont's *The Natural History of Love*. He incorporated into his own philosophy Gourmont's theory that sexual energy was the wellspring of the creative process. Ezra's specific thinking on the matter was sometimes tastelessly anatomical, but the link between sex and art would always interest him. Dorothy and Ezra had an unspoken agreement that he could have discreet affairs with the women who admired him whenever she was away.

Masterpieces

In the fall of 1921, T.S. Eliot stopped in Paris on his way back from medical leave at a sanitarium. Three months away from the bank had given him the time and space to finish his most ambitious poem yet: *The Waste Land*. He gave the first draft, which then totaled more than 40 pages, to Ezra for criticism and advice.

Ezra knew it was a masterwork from the first pages, but it was far from a finished piece of art. He recommended cuts that trimmed the poem's length by half. Eliot agreed with nearly all of these edits; recognizing the essential role that his friend had played in making *The Waste Land* what it was, Eliot dedicated the poem to Ezra, who still believed that his friend's enormous talents were being wasted at Lloyds Bank.

Early in 1922, Ezra resuscitated the plan to create a fund to allow Eliot to write without having to work a "day job." The plan was to recruit many subscribers, who would each pledge a small amount each year. Quinn pledged several hundred dollars. William Carlos Williams was slightly offended by the plan. He considered his medical practice to be his most important work. The idea of making poetry the focus of one's life seemed strange and unprofessional. Eliot felt much the same way. Ezra tried to keep the plan, known as Bel Esprit, a secret from his friend. When Eliot did find out, he denounced it, and begged the founders of Bel Esprit to stop.

Eliot wasn't the only writer producing masterpieces; in February 1922, Joyce's *Ulysses* was finally published in its entirety. Both *Ulysses* and *The Waste Land* were hugely inspirational for Ezra. He fed off the success and creative power of his friends to fuel his own work on *The Cantos*. But it was his translations of French poetry that was actually earning him a living at this point. New York's Boni and Liveright publishing house offered him a more than fair amount of money in exchange for more translations over the following two years.

Eager to repay his friend for editing *The Waste Land* so skillfully, Eliot asked Ezra if he would join the staff of his newly launched literary magazine, *The Criterion*. Ezra declined the offer, warning Eliot that ultimately, a magazine's financial backers dictated its contents, no matter how much freedom was promised to the editors. Although Eliot labored on his magazine for many years thereafter, Ezra turned out to be at least partially correct.

The year 1922 was full of important encounters when considered in hindsight. Early in the year, Ezra met the American reporter Ernest Hemingway. He was immediately fascinated by his youthful and masculine energy. Hemingway brought with him a letter of introduction from esteemed novelist Sherwood Anderson. He taught Ezra to box, and was a refreshing change of pace from his more "literary" friends. Later, Hemingway gave credit to Ezra as being one of the most important mentors of his career. Near the same time he met Hemingway, Ezra also began spending more time with Robert McAlmon, another expatriate writer whose tough-as-nails approach to realism was appealing to him.

Networking was vitally important in the publishing world: when Hemingway introduced Ezra to his publishing friend Bill Bird, it opened another door of opportunity. Bird had considered putting out a collection of classics under his imprint, but Ezra convinced him to instead release a collection of contemporary authors, to include himself and Hemingway, among others. Bird agreed, and the volumes he produced at Three Mountains Press were touchstones of Modernist literature.

In the spring, the Pounds vacationed once more in Italy. Dorothy returned sooner than her husband, leaving him to wander the familiar places at his own pace. After a decade of marriage and 15-plus years of knowing each other intimately, the Pounds were no longer passionate about each other. Friends of the couple had long remarked that Dorothy was cold and distant. Ezra had many flirtations and affairs during his marriage, believing in the power of sex to spur creativity, but the most important of these was with the violinist Olga Rudge. The pair met at Natalie Barney's salon, and sparks flew immediately.

1923

The Pounds organized a holiday dinner with the Yeatses and Joyces for Christmas 1922. Ezra had grown to despise the cold, drab Paris winter; Yeats suggested wintering in Italy in the future. Shortly thereafter, Ezra and Dorothy traveled to Rapallo, a sleepy and picturesque town on the Italian coast. Ezra was continuing to work on additions to *The Cantos*; no obvious stopping point had presented itself to him.

Hemingway and his wife Hadley joined Ezra and Dorothy later that winter. The group toured Italian battle sites from numerous wars. Hemingway was intimately familiar with those of the most recent war. By February, Ezra had made his way to the Vatican. Thanks to a Roman friend with connections, he was able to get access to the Holy City's archives and library; these documents aided him on *The Cantos* as well as his ongoing translation work.

In 1923, artists all over Europe, whether native or expatriate, felt an enormous pressure to take up a political position. World events had become too volatile for anyone to stand on the sidelines. France had occupied the Ruhr Valley; a fascist coup was underway in Spain; and Hitler was on the rise in Germany. In his own mind, Ezra was becoming more pessimistic about the world's fate. To combat his own insecurities, he invested even more faith in the apparently stabilizing power of fascist dictators.

Every stripe of radicalism was on the rise. Ezra became friends with the American Lincoln Steffens, and applauded loudly after his lecture on Soviet Russia. Both men agreed on the leadership prowess and commanding presence of the Italian Mussolini.

That spring, Dorothy made her annual trip to England to see her own family. But Ezra was not left alone: Olga Rudge was in town, as was his former patron John Quinn. Meanwhile Hemingway, who had returned temporarily to Toronto, sent him a letter warning him against a return across the Atlantic. He explained that Canada and the US were as uncultured as ever. Hemingway also encouraged his older friend to pay a visit to Gertrude Stein and Alice Toklas, but that encounter was a bust: Stein and Toklas were by turns amused and horrified by the carelessly energetic man who broke one of their chairs. For his part, Ezra found Stein completely boring.

In fact, Ezra was steadily becoming bored with Paris altogether. He wasn't such a young man anymore, and the endless hubbub of activity kept him from attending to his more serious work. Plus, he had built up the reputation of someone willing to lend a hand to others. So, he hatched a scheme to establish a small artist's colony in fascist Italy. Visitors to his apartment in summer 1923 recalled a person on the verge of mania or nervous breakdown.

Eliot did Ezra the service of publishing cantos 9 through 12 in the July issue of *The Criterion*. Distractions kept him from sustaining the positive momentum. Margaret Anderson introduced him to the experimental composer George Antheil, beginning a lengthy professional relationship, the first months of which were devoted to singing each other's praises in Paris newspapers. Ezra had no formal training in music, but that didn't stop him from producing his own opera and other musical arrangements. Together, Antheil and Ezra put the finishing touches on *Villon*, which had been half-finished for some time.

The advent of motion pictures was another fascinating distraction for Ezra, though the style and technique of film production eventually influenced the dizzying arrangement of *The Cantos*. By 1923, he had settled on 120 as the number of cantos he would write before declaring the project complete.

Ford Madox Ford came to Paris in the fall of 1923 to launch his new magazine. He intended the *transatlantic review* to pick up where the *English Review* had left off. To fill out the contents of the first few issues, he asked for contributions from Ezra, James Joyce, Hemingway, Gertrude Stein and e.e. cummings, among others. Ezra convinced Ford to make Hemingway his assistant editor. The magazine would not survive long, but it did provide an important outlet for Modernist writers of the 1920s.

Dorothy and Ezra traveled to Rapallo for the winter; Ezra's health was under attack from several directions. While in Italy, he firmly decided that his days in Paris were limited. Returning to the City of Lights in May, he almost immediately made preparations to leave, though it would be fall before the move could be arranged. In the meantime, a series of events confirmed in Ezra's mind the necessity of an exodus. At an artist's dinner, a crazed assailant tried to stab him. At the same time, his vocal support of the minor, reclusive, unhinged poet Ralph Cheever Dunning showed a lapse in his critical judgment. Friends and fellow artists didn't understand what was happening to the man they had known for so long as the manic but still rational Ezra Pound.

Chapter 4: Italy

Rapallo was the perfect setting for Ezra to concentrate on his cantos. Mountains and sea met dramatically, and tourists had yet to discover the small town of less than 15,000. After some brief hotel living, the Pounds took a terraced apartment on the waterfront.

Ezra and Dorothy didn't come to Italy alone; Olga Rudge, pregnant with Ezra's child, came too. Rudge believed her unborn child, conceived in Paris, constituted a mystical connection to the lover whom she adored. When Mary was born, she was adopted out to be raised by a peasant family in northern Italy. Perhaps out of a sense of competition, Dorothy became pregnant shortly afterwards. She had little serious interest in becoming a mother. Like Mary, Ezra's son Omar would be raised by others. In this case, his mother-in-law Olivia took the child as her own. Ezra was mostly oblivious to the lives of his children and their development.

Writing Into Obscurity

In January 1925, Three Mountains Press published most of the first 16 of *The Cantos*. What few reviewers noticed the event had nothing positive to say. Despite his own continued inability to stir the public imagination, Ezra lobbied on behalf of his closest friends as always. He composed a lengthy letter to New York's Guggenheim Foundation recommending that George Antheil, T.S. Eliot and Wyndham Lewis receive fellowship monies.

Meanwhile, a new magazine, *This Quarter*, began publication, and its editors communicated to Ezra that he would be a welcome contributor. They paid him reasonably well for his submission of cantos 17 through 19. Soon thereafter, he began to be bossy with the editors, suggesting what sort of direction the magazine ought to take, and they cut ties to him. Of course he wanted them to feature more economics and politics. Hemingway warned him that too much concentration on arcane knowledge, books and theories might sap his creative energies, if it hadn't already.

Winter and early spring 1926 was a relatively low-key period for Ezra; Dorothy was home nearly all the time, owing to her pregnancy. Ezra labored over canto 24. He took a brief trip to Paris to supervise the premiere of *Villon*, his opera that had been years in development. The critical reception was lukewarm at best; most said that in spite of pleasing arrangements, the subject matter was just too dense for the typical audience. It was one more in a line of failures and one more reason to think of the general public as unenlightened and incapable of appreciating his genius.

As summer came to Rapallo, Ezra devised a plan to start his own literary magazine. With no pressure from wealthy investors, he could lay out his whole philosophy, picking and choosing contributors from among those he admired. He may have been motivated by T.S. Eliot's recent launch of *The Criterion*. Since helping him to shape *The Waste Land* into a masterpiece, his relationship to his fellow American was complicated and often tinged with jealousy and spite. When Eliot took a job at Faber and Gwyer (later Faber and Faber, or just Faber), Ezra was even more annoyed – the job represented a dependable salary while keeping him in touch with the world of letters.

By January 1927, Ezra had secured enough funding to begin asking for contributions to *The Exile*. The title reflected in some sense how he felt about his place in the world. Rapallo was a world away from the literary centers of Paris and London. A typical day for Ezra consisted of writing in the morning, reviews and journalism later in the afternoon, and frequent breaks for walking, swimming, tennis, rowing and other physical pursuits. He was also keeping up on his background reading for *The Cantos*. When Yeats and Richard Aldington dropped in by surprise, all Ezra talked about was geopolitics and monetary policy. They couldn't make heads or tails of his conversation.

A steadily fading reputation drove Ezra to consider plans that he would have quickly dismissed only a few years earlier. For instance, he toyed with the idea of a lecture tour of the United States. He sensed – and others knew – that the new generation of writers did not count him as one of the literary elites. Few had even read him, and those that did pick up *The Cantos* were confused by its rapid jumps and cryptic allusions.

Old friends began turning their back on Ezra as his obsessions with economics and politics intensified. Late in 1927, Wyndham Lewis carries out a character assassination of him in *Time and the Western Man*. He accuses Ezra of living in the past and having a simplistic view of world events. Meanwhile, the writing style of *The Cantos* in the late 1920s reflected his disorganized and overstimulated mental state. The publication of the first issue of *The Exile* seemed to confirm Lewis's argument. The magazine was heavy with attacks on American culture, art, government and economic policy.

Still, Ezra was not without a few remaining admirers, despite his slide into obscurity. Marianne Moore lobbied successfully for him to receive the *Dial* Award, which included a cash prize of $2,000. Both Moore and T.S. Eliot applauded him in the January 1928 issue of *The Dial* that announced him as the winner. At the suggestion of respected scholar and publisher Glen Hughes, Ezra embarked on new translations of Confucius entitled *The Great Learning*. His work also began to appear more regularly in *The Dial*.

The *Dial* Award provided a temporary confidence boost for the poet. The mental block that had slowed his progress on *The Cantos* dissolved and work proceeded rapidly. Meanwhile, the publisher John Rodker agreed to print canto 17 through 27. In London, Eliot used his influence at Faber to publish Ezra's *Selected Poems*. In the spring, the third issue of *The Exile* was published. By this time, the magazine had complete devolved into a bullhorn for Ezra to shout his theories to anyone who was listening. The fourth issue would be the last.

After two decades of badgering their son about returning to America to find respectable work at a university, Ezra's parents decided to retire in Rapallo. The situation was both pleasant and worrisome. To ensure some degree of privacy for himself and Dorothy, he created a secret room within their apartment, tucked away behind a movable bookcase.

History, Politics and Fascism

On a whim, T.S. Eliot sent Ezra a multi-volume set of the works of Thomas Jefferson; they had been given to him as a gift, but he wasn't interested in Colonial American history at that point. Ezra, though, was captivated by the statesman's writings and theories. Many of these quickly surfaced in his cantos.

In spite of his new scholarly pursuit and artistic direction, Ezra's health deteriorated from late 1928 through the next year. He had previously suffered from digestive issues, and these returned with a vengeance. His mood also soured, probably an effect of the discomfort he was constantly enduring. Either way, he entertained few guests in 1929.

By the start of the new decade, Ezra felt healthy and stable enough to pay visits to both of his children. Between the two of them, he favored Mary. Omar was too closely associated with the aristocratic stuffiness of the Shakespear family. In Rapallo, however, he still did not go out of his way to invite visitors to his terraced apartment. When Yeats was in the region, Ezra deliberately avoided his old friend.

From his reclusive home by the sea, Ezra's nonfiction writing became increasingly angry and paranoid. An essay mercilessly attacking the character of America sent to *American Mercury* was instantly returned by its editor H.L. Mencken. In a letter to Ezra, Mencken argued that he was battling against an imaginary America. He suggested to the author of *The Cantos* that, having been an expatriate for most of two decades, he really ought to come visit the States and get a better sense of reality.

Beginning around 1930, Ezra launched an epic letter-writing campaign to men in positions of power in the United States. Presidents, Cabinet members, Congressmen and leaders of powerful organizations all heard from the expatriate poet at one point or another. Interestingly, he had begun dating his letters according to Italy's new fascist calendar, which marked 1922 as year 1. In many of these letters, he recommended a course of action to overcome the Great Depression, positioning himself as an expert on the subject matter of national economies. America (and the world's) economic freefall seemed to confirm all of his ideas about the way the world worked.

Ezra's central idea for remedying the Great Depression was for governments to borrow and then spend money – debt financing, in other words. The irony was lost on him that this would require more rather than less government intervention. It was an approach advocated by Maynard Keynes, the economist whose theories Ezra often railed against.

A few days before Ezra's 46th birthday in 1931, BBC Radio broadcast a performance of *Villon*. He was both shocked and fascinated. Much as people would later worry about TV over-consumption, Ezra worried that radio might invade everyone's home and take up all the world's free time. Still, he was intrigued by the medium's ability to reach a wide audience. He immediately saw how he could spread his own ideas about global politics if he only had a microphone in front of him.

In January 1932, a new set of Cavalcanti translations was published. Ezra wrote to the University of Pennsylvania to request he be awarded the doctorate; they refused, stating that he still had on-campus requirements to complete. This response reignited his distaste for the university system. Afterwards, his letters became even more bitter and hateful. When not writing spiteful letters, Ezra continued his exploration of American history. *Canto 34* presented material from *The Diary of John Quincy Adams*, among other sources.

Not everyone had written off Ezra Pound as crazy – his old associate A.R. Orage contacted him after founding *The New English Weekly* in London, asking for any contributions. The radical publication became a powerful mouthpiece for Ezra. Between 1932 and the start of the Second World War, he sent in almost 200 essays and reviews. At the same time, he was regularly sending pieces to Italian newspapers and magazines.

Ogden Nash, an editor at Faber, was also not scared off by Ezra's strange posturing. He had long been an admirer of *The Cantos*. He persuaded the firm to publish *A Draft of XXX Cantos*, the longest and most inclusive publication of Ezra's life work to date. Included in the collection were testimonials from Hemingway, Eliot, Joyce, H.D. and Archibald MacLeish.

In early 1933, Ezra finally had the opportunity to meet Benito Mussolini. Meeting the fascist dictator was a revelatory experience for the American poet. He didn't realize that Mussolini had not taken him seriously. Convinced of his own power and importance, Ezra began drafting a book comparing the dictator favorably with Thomas Jefferson. The meeting also had the unfortunate effect of encouraging him to become even more wrapped up in economic theories, geopolitics and social policy. That spring, Faber and Faber published *ABC of Economics*, Ezra's first book on the topic. The book was not without several good ideas, but it was bogged down by the weight of its bad ideas and overall disorganization.

Life in Rapallo had become a predictable and safe routine for the Pounds. Olga Rudge was also then living in the seaside community, and Ezra spent a few nights a week in her company. Dorothy was fully accepting of their unconventional marriage. Together, Ezra and Rudge were planning a concert series. A visit from Yeats in the summer of 1934 threw cold water on their friendship. Ezra ridiculed a play that the older poet had just completed; he was far more interested in political theater. Yeats wondered what had happened to the man he used to know.

War Looming

Anyone paying attention to European affairs in the mid-1930s could see that another war was on the horizon unless key players changed course. This was certainly not lost on Ezra – but his perspective on the root causes of war was different than most. He believed a triad of weapons manufacturers, banks and international financiers was responsible for all modern warfare. He both pitied and despised the ordinary citizens of nations for being so easily exploited.

In the fall of 1935, Italy invaded and occupied Ethiopia. Contradicting his own stance, Ezra felt the need to justify this attack. Winston Churchill had warned Mussolini that taking Ethiopia would be expensive and pointless; Mussolini, on the other hand, believed that war was a tool for boosting national pride and was a necessary element of any self-respecting fascist state.

Mussolini's son-in-law Count Galeazzo Ciano, who was appointed foreign minister of Fascist Italy, saw an opportunity to lend more credibility to Fascist Italy by having Ezra speak on Radio Rome. Ezra was given a lot of freedom to choose his own topics, and he not surprisingly gravitated toward economics and politics. His overt anti-Semitism became even more toxic, even in the context of the time period. He blamed Jews for the last war and the war to come, as well as the general decline of civilization. In private, though, he consistently denied having anti-Semitic beliefs. For most people, this contradiction was evidence of an unstable mind.

As the drumbeats of war grew louder, many of Ezra's American and English friends left Europe for the United States. Robert McAlmon, George Antheil and Ford Madox Ford all escaped the continent before all hell broke loose. Meanwhile, his harsh treatment of Yeats had repercussions. In a commentary on Ezra for his *Oxford Book of Modern Verse*, Yeats suggested that the poet had lost control of himself.

Ezra's most disorganized and confusing book yet, *Guide to Kulchur*, was released in 1937. He established no real thesis, and his arguments followed no logical order. Instead, he simply bounced from one disconnected idea to another. It was as if his conversational style had bled over into his writing process. Readers and critics who took notice of the book regarded it as more evidence of mental illness. Nevertheless, Ezra was soon thereafter elected to the National Institute of Arts and Letters in the United States.

The States were exercising a draw on Ezra as Europe rolled toward war. In Michigan, Ford had taken a distinguished teaching position at Olivet College. He wrote to Ezra to offer him a job there, his only responsibility being to mentor the most promising students. Because he didn't need money at the time and he knew how much he hated cold weather, he turned down the offer. A year later, Ford practically begged his old friend to come to Olivet and take over for him, but again he refused. Ford was possibly trying to get Ezra out of what would soon become a war zone.

In 1938, Ezra was revising cantos 53-61. These were based on both Chinese history and the life of John Adams, America's second president. As summer transitioned to fall, the dark shadow of war spread over the European continent.

World War II and The American Hour

Adolf Hitler and Neville Chamberlain signed their infamous non-aggression pact in September 1938. Ezra believed that England and the US were losing their position in the world and would soon be overtaken by the fascist powers of Europe. He ranked Mussolini and Hitler as the two greatest heads of state in the world.

Ezra had an interest in keeping the United States out of the coming war, though of course he had no power whatsoever to affect policy. His delusions of grandeur and omnipotence, however, convinced him to travel to Washington in April 1939. There, he tried and failed to gain an audience with Franklin Roosevelt. Instead, he was greeted by several Congressmen and Agriculture Secretary Henry Wallace. He implored them to avoid war at all costs and recommended some of his pet economic policies.

In May, Ezra traveled to New York and touched base with numerous friends – cummings, Ford and Lewis among them. He met long-time correspondents Marianne Moore and H.L. Mencken in person for the first time. His alma mater Hamilton College awarded him an honorary doctorate that June. Shortly before boarding the ship back to Italy, he visited Dr. Williams in New Jersey, where the two continued some of their old arguments.

After returning to Europe, Ezra sent cantos 52 through 71 to Faber for publication the following year. He also received the sad news that Ford had passed away. Outside of his poetry, Ezra began the slow descent into the kind of activities that would eventually see him charged with treason. In Italian and German fascist magazines and newspapers, he was actively denouncing America and its leaders. England was another target, but some of his most callous and hateful diatribes were reserved for people of Jewish descent.

On September 1, 1939, Germany invaded Poland in a swift ground attack. The Polish defenses might have been sturdy in the 19th century, but they were no match for tanks and heavy artillery. By the following spring, the other shoe dropped, and the German blitzkrieg was in full effect across Western Europe. Ezra considered another trip to the States, but wisely decided that trans-Atlantic travel was likely too dangerous by then.

War naturally slowed Ezra's work on *The Cantos*, but his output of letters and articles increased dramatically. A friend in Rapallo named Uberti introduced him to the Fascist Confederation of Artists. The FCA then connected Ezra to the Italian Ministry of Popular Culture, which hosted a series of radio programs, among other official duties. The Ministry was interested in giving the poet an audience provided he could discourage the United States from joining the conflict. And they had just the platform from which he might do just that: a regular broadcast called *The American Hour*. By this point, the FBI had begun monitoring Ezra's political writings and statements. The radio shows would be exponentially more damaging.

Ezra's first *American Hour* radio broadcast was in January 1941. From then on, pre-recorded broadcasts hit the airwaves about every three days. He was also responsible for writing scripts for other programs, press releases, and any other needed material. Ezra was an important cog in the propaganda machine, and he was well compensated for these efforts.

Italian audiences, though, never fully comprehended what Ezra was trying to communicate. Much like his conversation and recent books, his presentations were rambling and confused. When America officially joined the war after the attack on Pearl Harbor, he temporarily left the radio. Someone had warned him that given the new state of affairs, *The American Hour* broadcasts could easily be viewed as treason by his home nation. The American Embassy then instructed any nationals still in Italy to leave, but the Italian military gave the Pound family special permission to remain in the country.

The radio show resumed, and Ezra's voice could be heard twice a week. In the States, the FBI was visiting all of his friends and acquaintances to build up a profile of the expatriate poet. William Carlos Williams, e.e. cummings and Archibald MacLeish all gave information to the agency. Ezra was officially indicted for treason on July 26, 1943.

Summer 1943 was a turning point in the conflict. Germany had been pushed out of North Africa, and the Italian peninsula was obviously vulnerable. Sicily was the first part of the country to be taken by the Allies. Ezra knew that the walls were closing in on him. He wrote an impassioned letter to the US Attorney General to justify his actions, citing free speech as his shield against the charge of treason.

The fascist Italian government essentially ceased functioning by the fall of 1943, and German forces swooped in to fill the power vacuum and provide security to the Reich's southern borders. Ezra and Dorothy moved in with Olga as German warships patrolled the coast of Rapallo. With the situation going from bad to worse, Ezra headed out on foot to see his daughter Mary in the north of the country. He arrived in an almost unrecognizable state.

The Germans established a puppet regime in northern Italy. Even at this late hour, Ezra was not fully convinced that the governments he had so strongly stood behind could falter. His radio propaganda continued from Milan, only now he was only writing scripts. His few remaining friends in America all agreed that he had totally lost his wits.

The End

The Pounds were living in Rapallo again by early spring, with Ezra making regular commutes to the German base of operations in Milan. On May 1, American soldiers occupied the seaside town, facing no resistance to speak of. Photos of Ezra had been circulated by the military, but no one in Rapallo recognized him at first. Ezra even volunteered to help the soldiers, suggesting that his knowledge of the country would be a benefit in their campaign. On May 2, a couple of locals believed they could earn a reward by capturing the poet and handing him over to the Americans.

Military police offers transported Ezra to Genoa for processing. He was interrogated before being moved on to a detention center in Pisa. There, he was held in a stockade and received no special treatment. For weeks on end, he lived in a 6 by 6 foot steel and concrete cell that offered little protection from the elements. With no human interaction, he mentally and physically succumbed to the ordeal after three weeks.

Officers moved the broken poet to the center's medical facility, where he was questioned by a group of psychiatrists over the course of several days. They recommended that a hospital in the United States would better be able to care for him. Lieutenant Colonel John Steele negated that recommendation. Instead, Ezra was given somewhat more freedom within the detention center. He was allowed to write again and to move around at will. In October, he received a visit from Dorothy. Mary and Olga Rudge visited shortly thereafter. Then, on November 16, 1945, Ezra boarded a military transport to Washington to face charges of treason.

Chapter 5: Washington

Ezra Pound arrived in the nation's capital on November 18; he begged for the right to defend himself but was denied. His attorney, Julien Cornell, recommended an insanity plea. Most people who saw Ezra around this time could understand how such a plea might be successful. At his November 27 arraignment, the judge ordered that he be removed to a hospital for psychiatric examination.

Four different psychiatrists interviewed Ezra through December, led by Dr. Winfred Overholser. The consensus among the doctors was that their patient was unfit to stand trial. From there, Ezra was sent to St. Elizabeth's Hospital, a federally run mental health facility, for an indefinite amount of time. It was the beginning of a profound period of limbo for the poet. Should he at any point be judged sane, he would be brought to trial and almost certainly face life in prison or a death penalty. On the other hand, if the psychiatrists maintained that he was mentally unwell, he could be a resident of St. Elizabeth's for the rest of his life.

In early 1946, a final sanity hearing was held. The jury quickly decided that the Ezra's mind was unsound. He was housed in Howard Hall, the prison ward, for his first several years at St. Elizabeths. On the outside, public opinion was solidly against him. There were whispers that Dr. Overholser was at the head of a conspiracy to save the poet from his inevitable fate. Ezra's was the first treason case brought by the United States in the wake of World War II. Meanwhile, in Howard Hall, Ezra played games with the psychiatrists; he had no faith in the psychological sciences and felt he could outsmart his interviewers.

Ezra received few visitors in what he called the "hell hole." Mencken and Eliot were among his first and only guests. Another was the younger writer Charles Olson. Dorothy had to jump through bureaucratic hoops to get her passport renewed and her funds unfrozen, but she finally arrived in Washington in June. His oldest friend of all, William Carlos Williams, felt little sympathy, reportedly saying that he got what he deserved.

After the November elections, Cornell felt the time was right to work toward Ezra's release. He argued that it was unconstitutional to hold someone indefinitely without a trial, regardless of an insanity finding. If Ezra would never be mentally capable of standing trial, but was no real danger to himself and other, then he ought to be set free, or so the case went. Cornell's appeal was rejected in both 1947 and 1948.

Living conditions did improve somewhat when Ezra was moved to his own room just down the hall from Dr. Overholser. From his single window, he could look out on the Library of Congress. He was even allowed to stroll the grounds and hold a kind of "salon" in the ward. More and more people came to see the poet, and slowly but surely, opinions about what ultimately should be done with him began to change. Dorothy, having taken a small apartment in the city, visited every day. Ezra began to write again, picking up where he left off on *The Cantos* and composing long letters for friends. After an unofficial embargo, important journals like *Poetry* and the *Sewanee Review* started to print his latest works.

Despite everything that had happened, Ezra still held on to his pre-war racist and anti-Semitic philosophies. Friends couldn't reason with him on these points. To counteract his dangerous stubbornness, T.S. Eliot spearheaded an effort to nominate Ezra for the first-ever Bollingen Award. *The Pisan Cantos*, composed while confined in Italy and only recently published, represented perhaps the most perfect lyrics that he had ever produced; most of his friends felt that he was more than deserving of the award. However, the Bollingen committee proceeding was not without controversy: two members strongly objected to giving the award to an accused traitor. Ezra's allies knew that if he received the award, the Justice Department would be in a ticklish situation. Mencken suggested in a letter to the attorney general that the poet might be in the running for Nobel Prize in the near future.

Enormous efforts were underway to get Ezra released before he died at the hospital. A serious respiratory illness in 1953 seemed to confirm the need for haste. Politically, though, the support for clemency just wasn't there yet. When Ernest Hemingway won the Nobel Prize in 1954, he remarked that the award could easily have gone to Ezra.

Popular opinion on Ezra had shifted by the middle of the 1950s. The war was ten years in the past, and his supposedly treasonous activities did not seem so heinous in hindsight. Eliot petitioned Eisenhower for his release; Archibald MacLeish was Ezra's most vocal supporter. He asked Robert Frost, then the nation's most famous poet, to intercede on Ezra's behalf. Everything appeared to be moving in the right direction. The only question that the authorities had was how the poet planned to support himself if he should be released.

At a hearing on April 19, 1958, Ezra was granted his freedom, and he left St. Elizabeth's on May 7. After a few weeks of visiting his friends and supporters, he and Dorothy boarded a ship bound for Italy on June 30. When he disembarked, he gave the fascist salute, announcing that perhaps he had changed very little in the course of his 13-year incarceration.

Chapter 6: Last Years in Italy

Ezra Pound was 72 years old when he came to Italy to live out his final years. Joining him were his wife Dorothy and his secretary and devoted admirer Marcella Spain, a former schoolteacher from Texas and 40 years his junior. He met his young grandchildren, Walter and Patrizia, for the first time. They had both been born while he was at St. Elizabeths.

Advanced years and fatigue did not at first prevent Ezra from continuing work on his cantos. At that point, he was revising material that he had written while under psychiatric confinement. He called cantos 96 through 109 the "Thrones" section. His feistiness was limited by chronic neck and back pain; the Alpine air of northern Italy made his breathing labored, and he dreaded the cold and snowy winters.

Domestically, the convergence of Marcella with Dorothy and Mary was a source of unrelenting tension. Ezra had become infatuated with Marcella, provoking jealousy in both his daughter and his wife. Dorothy and Mary were also jealous of each other and possessive of their patriarch. In the spring of 1959, Ezra, his wife and Marcella returned to Rapallo and rented an apartment. Olga Rudge had already been there for some time. That May, a grand tour of Italy included a visit to the site of the detention center in Pisa, which had long been converted into a rose garden.

According to the terms of his release from St. Elizabeth's, Dorothy had guardianship of Ezra and control of his finances and legal affairs. After her husband mentioned that he was thinking of divorce, Dorothy made peace with Mary so as to push Marcella out of the inner circle. She returned to America, and Ezra was depressed and feeling powerless.

Ezra's mood in Italy became one of darkness and fatigue, punctuated by short bursts of energy. He also became noticeably silent, not even speaking with many of his visitors. Privately, he wondered if *The Cantos* had been a waste of time. His paranoia increased, and he was wracked by fears of persecution, sickness, insanity and death. Probably feeding these fears was the inevitable passing of many of his lifelong friends. Wyndham Lewis had died in 1957. Hemingway took his own life in 1961. e.e. cummings passed the next year, and Williams the year after that. T.S. Eliot, one the last bastions of the Modernist generation, died in 1965. Ezra traveled to London to deliver a short eulogy in Westminster Abbey.

In the summer of 1960, Ezra all but stopped eating and drinking. Dorothy transported him to a clinic before he could starve to death. By summer's end, he was recovered enough to be discharged, and his spirits seemed outwardly improved. But his inner depression and doubt had not evaporated. Elderly herself, Dorothy realized she was no longer able to care for her husband to the degree he needed. She therefore handed his care over to Olga Rudge in 1961. Dorothy moved to England to spend her twilight years with her and Ezra's son, Omar.

Ezra's apartment became a mecca for younger poets touring Europe. He was visited by Allen Ginsberg in 1967. During their meeting, Ezra was mostly quiet. Reportedly, he did remark to Ginsberg that his anti-Semitism was his biggest regret. TV shows and reporters came in droves, eager to speak with the last living Modernist poet, but Ezra was notoriously silent. It was a complete about-face from his youthful talkative self. In the fall of 1972, he had become all but bedridden. He did summon the strength to give a reading from *The Cantos* prior to his 87th birthday.

Ezra Pound died in his sleep the day after his birthday celebration. Olga arranged the simple funeral, and he was buried in Venice on November 1.

Conclusion

Ezra Pound was one of the most controversial figures in 20th century English literature. Much of this controversy was self-generated, as he had a notorious inability to censor himself. This was most obvious during the Second World War. Whether he truly regretted his Italian radio broadcasts after his confinement in St. Elizabeth's is unknown. Either way, history has been kind to his cultural reputation. For most of his youth, Ezra wished to be directing the course of the arts; later, he hoped to shape world events, a tragic mistake.

Bibliography

"Ezra Pound." (n.d.) *Academy of American Poets*. http://www.poets.org/poetsorg/poet/ezra-pound

"Ezra Pound in His Time and Beyond." (2009). *University of Delaware Library*. http://www.lib.udel.edu/ud/spec/exhibits/pound/translation.htm

"Ezra Pound recordings." (2006). *PENNSOUND*. http://writing.upenn.edu/pennsound/x/Pound.php

The Ezra Pound Society. (2014). http://ezrapoundsociety.org/index.php/works

Goodwin, K.L. (1966). *The Influence of Ezra Pound*. Oxford University Press.

Heymann, C. David. (1976). *Ezra Pound, the Last Rower: A Political Profile*. New York: Viking Press.

Tryphonopoulos, D.P. and Stephen Adams. (2005). *The Ezra Pound Encyclopedia*. Westport, CT: Greenwood Press.

Tytell, John. (1987). *Ezra Pound: The Solitary Volcano*. New York: Doubleday.

Printed in Great Britain
by Amazon.co.uk, Ltd.,
Marston Gate.